78 N.L.

To my imaginary
lover Miss Eli —
Anthony

Voyage Into Solitude

Voyage Into Solitude

Michael Dransfield

Collected and edited by
Rodney Hall

University of Queensland Press

Also by Michael Dransfield:

Streets of the Long Voyage
The Inspector of Tides
Drug Poems
Memoirs of a Velvet Urinal

Published by University of Queensland Press, St. Lucia,
Queensland, 1978

Distributed in the United Kingdom, Europe, the Middle
East, Africa, and the Caribbean by Prentice-Hall
International, International Book Distributors Ltd.,
66 Wood Lane End, Hemel Hempstead, Herts., England

Published with the assistance of the Literature Board
of the Australia Council

National Library of Australia
Cataloguing-in-Publication data
Dransfield, Michael, 1948–1973.
  Voyage into solitude.

  ISBN 0 7022 1246 6 Paperback.
  ISBN 0 7022 1245 8.

  1. Hall, Rodney, 1935– , ed. II. Title

A821'.3

CONTENTS

INTRODUCTION

Assembling the manuscripts

Michael Dransfield was astonishingly gifted. By the age of nineteen he was already writing mature poems and, in the extremely conservative context of Australian literature, these were poems which announced a colourful, exotic presence. He was also prolific. He wrote compulsively, often five or six poems a day. Even for those of us who knew him, it sometimes seemed doubtful that he had any kind of life outside poetry. Yet of course he did, his friends and his interests were numerous. One of the great assets of Michael Dransfield's life was that the people he mostly lived among accepted him as a poet right from the start. His friends *expected* him to write poems –how different from the experience of most poets who pursue their craft almost as a clandestine activity and who often feel they must do their best to persuade the respectable community (and perhaps themselves) of their passionate interest in cars, beer and football, even if they have no such interest. The kind of acceptance Michael had among his peers was a tremendous liberation and spur to his creative energies. The free-ranging tone of the poems, and this applies to the very earliest poems as well, must be seen as partly a product of this sub-culture where to be a poet was (and still is) nothing so very strange— and certainly blameless in a society seen to be blameworthy in most of its aspects and most of its activities.

Michael did not accept this situation passively, however, he was too ambitious for that. He was already over the next hurdle before he came to it. It was characteristic of him that in the Acknowledgments list of his book *Drug Poems*, the last entry reads: ' " I Do This I Do That" will appear in *Memoirs of a Velvet Urinal* to be published in the USA in 1972'. It never was. The most he had was an offer from Geoffrey Dutton in Adelaide to take the manuscript with him to America and see if he could interest anyone in it. Of course, this was a recipe for disappointment; despite his many successes they were never enough to match his expectations, nor even to make good his claims.

During the years I knew him well, Michael could always be depended on to have a clutch of books assembled and ready for publication. At any time he might announce that he had, say, three new volumes of poems, a novel and, perhaps, a biography of Henry Purcell all but ready. If anything, this puts it too modestly. For example, in 'Psalm' he himself sums up his possessions as:

> nametags left in a cloakroom
> ten unpublished books some letters
> the possessions one acquires
> on a visit to this planet

He needed those books. And, at least as far as the collections of poetry were concerned, they existed right enough. The prose works were another matter and more in the nature of whimsical projects until the last six months of his life when he really did get a fair amount written of a novel in the form of a diary, to be called *Jack*.

So when, within days of his death, I began the task of collecting and saving as much of his work as I could, I knew there would be a lot of it. For a start, we had a box full which he always housed at our place. Then word got round and many of his friends sent in bundles of poems and letters. A special debt of gratitude is owing to Ann Buddle and Richard Hopkinson who gathered a great deal of material, notes and typescripts, and without whom many of these poems might well have been lost for ever.

The manuscripts were finally assembled in 1976 after three years' work and put together with those held by the poet's mother, Mrs Elspeth Dransfield, plus copies of poems lodged with the National Library in Canberra and the Fryer Library at the University of Queensland. Altogether we gathered over six hundred poems, nearly all written during the six years from mid-1967 to March 1973.

When I first agreed to edit this book, my idea was to publish everything that could be found and thus allow the work to find its own level. But of course sheer bulk made this impracticable. So I have had to take the plunge and exclude many poems from my selection. Doubtless, subsequent editors will make good any mistakes of judgment. And their job will be substantially easier as all the poems are now typed up and will be made available for future research.

In introducing this book I think I can claim to have special experience in editing Michael's poetry. He began sending me poems at the *Australian* in 1967. The first batch surprised and displeased me with their Keatsian lushness, yet they could not be overlooked. I wrote to this unknown author explaining why I wasn't accepting his poems and suggesting where I thought their strengths and weaknesses lay. A couple of days later a long and furious reply arrived, stating that people of his generation had something to say too, didn't I realize, and what right had I to ignore the merits of his poetry and so forth—the letter was signed, incongruously it seemed, with warm thanks for my interest. Such passionate involvement in what he was doing I found irresistibly attractive. Of course I wrote again; and so a correspondence began and a friendship which was only cut short by his death.

There is a sad kind of symmetry for me in presenting this posthumous collection, because I had the privilege of being closely involved in the selection of poems that went into his first book, *Streets of the Long Voyage.*

Voyage into Solitude is half of a two-volume set, and represents a selection of poems previously uncollected in book form, covering the period 1967–71. Volume two, to be called *The Second Month of Spring,* will cover the period 1972–73.

A poet against mechanarchy

Michael Dransfield died on Good Friday 1973. He was twenty-four years old. At the time he had published three books of poems and was already something of a cult-hero among young people who shared his anger against the callous commercialism of our society and his experience as a drug addict. He spoke for many who had never had a voice before. There is no doubt they loved him for it—and still do. I think it would be true to say that he and the Aboriginal poet Kath Walker are the only Australian poets of recent times with a genuine popular following, a following among people who do not otherwise read poetry.

And yet his poems never talk down to people nor assume the modesty of prose. In most respects his mode is High Romantic, his vocabulary of images at times positively gothic. But, unlikely as it may appear, these very characteristics contribute to his popular appeal: the desire for vivid, colourful, and fantastic notions being so much part of the world of the 'alternative society'. His use of archaic spellings, the abundance of viols and lutes, tapestries, princes and sundry enchantments is understood in terms of fancydress because of the brutal, despairing context from which so much of his poetry speaks: it is what the poet actually says that raises both the quaintness and the squalor to the level of moving (even rhapsodic) poetry.

Reviewers and critics have already paid some attention to Courland Penders, that ramshackle abandoned family homestead, parts of which are described in all his books. There has been some earnest rooting around for evidence as to whether it was 'real' or 'imaginary'. Surely this is not the point. He *needed* Courland Penders for his imaginative balance, it was a tool for the survival of his imagination. It was his ideal. And if justice were to be done to his sense of history, his tastes, his passions, a Courland Penders would have been his. Even its dilapidation is important to the romantic aura of the place:

> twenty rooms four thousand acres
> emptiness and desolation

as he writes of it in an unpublished poem 'Courland Penders: Reminiscences'.

Fancydress implies playing a part; of course he played a part. And most of all he enjoyed exploring the public image of a Poet. . .still, astonishingly enough the Keats/Shelley model. This suited him for he shared with the nineteenth century romantics a belief that history is created by individuals, that our history was made by Caesar and Elizabeth I, Dante and Marx, James Cook, St Augustine and Napoleon, not the faceless people, much less those abstractions class and capital—nothing so impersonal as the collective need for food or greed for wealth; but the passion and energy of the gifted individual.

He survived experiences that might well have killed off a good many of his detractors. He earned his fanciful words and his wishful thinking in terms of the poetry he made of them. It was one of his hobbies to toy with the idea of remote nobility among his ancestors on both his mother's and his father's side (Pender and Dransfield). The furnishing of an old family house, physical embodiment of his cultural inheritance was one of the ways he managed to survive. In 1969 he commented 'I'm the ghost haunting an old house, my poems are posthumous'.

There are few enough of these baronial pieces, all said and done; for the most part the poetry is essentially a diary. A glance through this book will show how many of the poems begin with the day, the morning, the evening, the night, his room, names of friends and lovers—commentaries on how his time was spent and with whom, what they did and thought, what they saw and the reactions of those who watched them. He is perfectly open about this:

> preserving his identity through friends,
> 'the poet as the letter X', resisting
> all but the past because that never ends.
> He seemed to build a labyrinth consisting
> of everything he loved, that distance rends
> and passion clouds with fateful nearness. . .
>
> (from 'Death as triumph')

Some poems, like 'Peter' give explicatory autobiographical details which help clarify the threads running throughout the fabric of Michael Dransfield's poetry.

The diary poems are devastatingly frank. He may wear motley dress, but never a mask. He says things about himself which must have taken immense courage to say. Small wonder that the 'real' world could seem so unbearable and hallucinations so alluring. Just how he judged this aspect of life was clearly put in 'That which we call a rose', first published in the *Australian* in 1969, mourning the death of two young friends, Rick and George:

> One dead of hunger the other of overdose their
> ideals precluded them
> from the Great Society

It might be pointed out here that one of the distinguishing features of Michael Dransfield's poems about the experience of taking drugs is that they are not content to be just drug poems: more often they are an attempt to place the individual in society, or else a means of relating the past to the present through dreamlike elisions. There can be no doubt that he felt a fellowship with the victims of our system whether these were individual criminals or an entire outmoded social order. Also in the *Australian* he published a letter of appreciation for the series *Poems from Prison*, in which he had this to say:

> . . . Yes. The victims of our society, the outcast,
> the imprisoned, are articulate. That is the history
> of art.
> The view through a cell window has a perfect
> and terrible inevitability. Always the guilty go free.
> It's their game, they own the wars . . .
>
> (17 July 1972)

Just so his beloved aristocracy fell victim to capital, having been dealt its fatal blow by the very same Industrial Revolution which gave birth to the machine age, mechanarchy and computerdom, which lie at the heart of the social impotence and aimlessness suffered so generally by youth today. Michael was among those who felt this social impotence and longed to escape it into dreams and poetry. But he also nursed a fiery conviction that dreams and poems could be used as a weapon of defiance. He saw himself as having a mission to undermine mechanarchy by spreading his ideas about beauty and love and art. So in this respect too he resisted every demand that he be a stable respectable member of this Great Society. He made himself an outsider and stayed that way, constantly on the move, renting a flat here, buying an old house there, but always moving, selling, hitch-hiking, riding his motorbike, staying with friends and relatives, moving on. The theme of leaving is reiterated throughout this collection. And though it carries with it the overtones of loss and alienation, what he really feared was the closing of exits. This idea is superbly put in 'Partita' with its window becoming a mirror and therefore rejecting him by rejecting his projection of vision, giving him back not the world outside, the world of leaving, but only himself, dissatisfaction, the limiting and rigid confines of the room. The voyage to solitude has much to do with this transformation of the window into the mirror: the outward-looker becoming the inward-looker. In 'Chaconne for a Solipsist' the image is explicit and is used with grim exultation.

Notes on the selection

In this book, as in Michael Dransfield's previous publications there are not many themes, though he discovered many ways of approaching them. Like most poets, he was obsessed by a few themes. So it is not surprising in a collection which he did not have the opportunity of culling and polishing for himself, that there are many recurrent images —and even re-used lines. Where it seems to me that two poems each make strong and valid use of the same line, I have included them both, though it may very well be that one was discarded by the author in favour of the other, and the choice line(s) lifted for use in the new context. So it is that 'Form' and 'Outing' end respectively with the lines:

> the absolute centre of a
> Civilization is something which rots

and:

> the true
> centre of time is something
> which rots

so also 'In the high country' ends with the haunting lines:

> old men's feet make
> promises
> on midnight roads

exactly the same idea crops up again (and I suspect a little earlier) in the middle of 'And no bird sings: autumn breaks on high rocks'

> & old men's feet
> make promises on
> midnight roads

Another of these images is the black bird, that ancient symbol of death, sitting at the window or captured in a mirror, with white clouds massed at its head like snow, like dreams, as in 'Dear Charles' and 'Illness'. There are plenty more examples for those who wish to hunt them out. Similarly he re-used titles: titles of a kind which tell their own story, as with 'Journal d'un homme vide' and 'And no birds sing'.

Of course there does come a point where too much of a poem is borrowed from or lent to other, superior poems. Some quite publishable pieces I have left out, because they are so much part of others, and seem to be no more than the working out of ideas more fully expressed elsewhere. Often his method of revision did give rise to versions that look almost like separate poems. As an example of this I am including three drafts of a poem originally called 'Satie' with notes made by the author (see Appendix A).

The compilation of a posthumous collection is a daunting responsibility, precisely because of the finality of form in the work as it's left standing.

So among the six hundred poems there were some which I found difficult to exclude whereas, had Michael been alive still, I might have had no hesitation in recommending him to scrap them. These are the poems containing one good line, one or two startling images, one extraordinary perception, but little else. A posthumous collection must, I believe, bear in mind the importance of salvaging work unjustly overlooked. Every single one of the poems in this volume had been written in time for inclusion in the books the author published during his lifetime. Fortunately for me (and I hope for the reader) Michael was not a particularly good editor of his own work; in assembling his books he discarded quite a lot of fine poems which are collected here for the first time. It is astonishing to think of 'Sonnet', for example, being left out of anyone's book. The best poems are of very high quality indeed.

As I have already mentioned, he was forever shuffling the poems about and assembling them into putative collections. Frankly, I think this interfered with his clarity of judgment about them; he came to think of certain poems as belonging in groups. This was the case in *Memoirs of a Velvet Urinal* where quite a few poems are included which fall well below the general standard of the others (this is true even in the version of the manuscript held by the Fryer Library, which is later than the one published by Maximus Books).

Apart from the mass of miscellaneous manuscripts, three hard-bound collections were consulted for the present selection: these were titled *'The Cocklebiddy Fisherman'*, *'Abdication'*, and *'The Bible as Fiction'*. They are each of a kind familiar to Michael's friends and editors—collections he was constantly engaged in assembling and which were at various times abandoned and dismantled in favour of those books he did in fact publish. *'The Cocklebiddy Fisherman'* is available to be consulted in the Fryer Library at the University of Queensland and *'The Bible as Fiction'* is in the National Library. The exact content of *'Abdication'* is not now known, I think, but the title page, the dedication and a jumble of its pages were found in a folder among his papers.

Notes on the order, editing and presentation of the poems

Another decision which had to be taken concerned the order of the poems as they appear in this book. There were two main possibilities; to arrange them chronologically, or to arrange them as a collection (shaped so that they complement one another and cohere as a statement). I chose the latter. It wasn't a hard decision. For a start, though most of the poems are dated exactly, even to the minute they were finished, some have no dates at all; and even with surmised dates for these poems, the book as a whole looked haphazard and patchy when arranged chronologically. I felt there was far more to be brought out in it than that. So, although the earlier poems are mainly at the beginning and the later poems mainly at the end (as this underlines the point of the title), the order in all other respects is entirely imposed by me and whatever fault may be found with it is to be laid at my door not Michael Dransfield's.

Some of the poems in manuscript carry appendages like footnotes. Where these seem to me to add to the poem I have included them at the foot of the page. Where they are extraneous (often the manuscripts are part of letters to friends, for instance) I have left them out.

Whether or not to include dates with the poems posed another decision. Personally I find it intrusive and distracting to have *9.XII.1970:11.50pm. Marchpane* *, or something of the sort tagged on to a poem which has moved me, a decision Michael himself made in all three books he published during his lifetime. But obviously there is an interest in the dates. Accordingly, a key to the year of composition is provided as Appendix B; where no available copy of the poem gives a date, dates have surmised and are listed as such.

---

* How characteristic that his favourite among the houses he bought, a modest old timber place at Cobargo, NSW, he named 'Marchpane', (the Elizabethan word for marzipan icing!).

Having arranged the book as a statement rather than a chronology, one of the resultant curiosities is to be seen in the punctuation used. In his later poems Michael dispensed with punctuation altogether, using line-endings and mid-line spaces instead. In a few of the revised versions of earlier poems he set them out in this way also. I have not interfered at all at any point with the latest version of each manuscript that could be found. Thus, several systems of layout and punctuation are employed in this book. The sequence "Poem about the sun" is a case in point as the last part of the sequence can only be found in an earlier draft than the rest.

The same rule has been applied to eccentricities of spelling. However, in one poem "No forwarding address", the word 'impassible' (line 31) does seem to be a spelling error rather than an intentional elision of two words, simply because the elision would be too weak to make its point. I take 'impassable' to be the intended word rather than 'impossible'. Naturally, there were innumerable decisions of this kind which had to be taken by Mrs Elspeth Dransfield when she was making the first typescript from those poems existing only in handwritten form. I might say here that a special tribute is owing to her on several accounts: firstly that she has dedicated herself to many months' work on deciphering scrawls of handwriting, deciphering which perhaps no one outside the family could have achieved so completely, and secondly that she has been able to face the enormous emotional strain of preparing the typescript—even from the sample selected for this volume (a mere one hundred and twenty of the six hundred) it will be clear how very distressing this experience must have been for the poet's mother in terms of what Michael says about his own life.

The right to publish the poems here is on Mrs Dransfield's authority.

The poet's style and influences

Michael Dransfield's reputation is already secure enough not to need confirmation here, but I will perhaps add a footnote which might be interesting to readers of the poems which follow. Various persons (perhaps attracted by a desire to be associated with the public image of Michael as a doomed innocent, a tragic figure, a free spirit) have claimed special knowledge of what Michael said about influences on his life and work. Most of it, true or not, is repeated at the level of gossip. And to some extent I believe it is a fact that Dransfield the public figure does tent to obscure Dransifeld the poet. People are always asking who one's favourite poet is; and the answer may well be misleading.

I think it is helpful to bear in mind the distinction between stance and style—the stance of the poet *as* poet, and the style of the poetry itself. The one is to do with the poet's self-image, the other is to do with the workable vocabulary of form he inherits from the tradition. Michael Dransfield's stance was essentially that of a romantic: the poet as hero figure, with what I've already called 'the need to believe that history is created by individuals'. In the matter of stance, at his back stand Keats and Swinburne. But as for style, he was the inheritor of modern poetry in many languages. The way was opened for Michael by Salvatore Quasimodo. The Penguin Books translation of this poet's work became an important touchstone for Michael's development of a style he could really use. The ending of Quasimodo's poem 'And your dress is white' shows this clearly enough:

The road was deep
that the wind went down
certain March nights,
and woke us unknown
like the first time.

Another example from the same collection is 'Ancient
winter', a poem I shall always associate with Michael,
as we sat one whole afternoon in the garden of my
house in Brisbane reading the poem to each other over
and over and discussing it:

Desire of your bright
hand in the flame's half-light;
flavour of oak, roses
and death

Ancient winter.

The birds seeking the grain
were suddenly snow.

So words:
a little sun; a haloed glory,
then mist; and the trees
and us, air, in the morning.

He wasn't the only one to be influenced by Quasimodo.
It is frequently claimed that Michael Dransfield's style
was unique, but I do not think any such claim can be
sustained. What made the poems unique was the use
he put this style to: his combination of style and
stance, creating a sort of fancy-dress diary on one hand
and a savage cosmology of the hallucinatory universe
on the other. After all, a clear ten years before Michael
discovered this style for himself another Australian poet
Don Maynard was using a style almost identical, as

styles go. Michael was still in primary school when this Maynard poem was published:

Sub-tropical

this always was the season
for coming to grips
this seaside sticky weather
for the senses

lying under a bosom moon
feeling centreboard
feeling the shell-oil waves
breaking the toes of sand/& the soft centre
                              of the palm
                              of your hand
                              under the hot moon

Somewhere between stance and style lies the process of how a poem is triggered off, the working method. Here his debt was beyond doubt to Rainer Maria Rilke. Though there's little similarity between Rilke's object-poetry and Michael's cartography of his feelings, he knew Rilke from schooldays. He once discussed with me Rilke's own account of how Rodin had sent him out to 'see' in order to write, at a time when the poet was Rodin's secretary—the first (superb) fruit of this method being Rilke's 'The Panther'. Michael himself in his diary-poems set out daily to 'see' in much this way.

I think the only poet who ever offered Michael a model in that total sense as poet and person whom he could identify with and, if you like, envy—was Rimbaud. The reassurance he found in identifying with Rimbaud had much to do with age, with the fact that all Rimbaud's poetry was written by the time he was nineteen, that he was the very figure of a genius at the same time surviving a life of squalor. Also that he survived with the capacity to laugh still and to treat orthodox decorum with a fine disdain.

Michael himself never lost the humour to laugh at the world and himself. He was talkative and vivacious, he loved jokes and games with words, and he had an insatiable craving for eccentric knowledge. In the last months of his life, when he could no longer concentrate to read books, this was one of his great compensations, he slipped easily into the oral tradition of storytellers— likewise, I believe, there is evidence in the contrast between this volume and the next of how his poetry developed from poems for the eye to poems for the ear.

R.H.
Bermagui
19.vii.77

Don Maynard's poem *Sub-tropical* was originally published in *Four Poets* published by Cheshire (Melbourne) in 1962.

And all the world

a picture of me as a priest
for who we are is what we leave
and all the world is my estate
the clouds and castles and the sun
let this be how my poems are
pieces of sandstone bleached by light
a wineglass filled with what you see
when wine is blood in seeing's veins

to be printed as the first and introductory poem to the book *Abdication*
3.X.69 7.55pm for Hilary

Sonnet

"And he may never dare again say what awaits him, or be sure
what sunlit labyrinth of pain he may not enter and endure."
                                   —from 'Hillcrest', E.A. Robinson

Needing to speak. Just that. Even if no-one listens.
Saying something to drive back for a second the immense silence.
The voice a gull falling below a cliff/fading immediately/was it there?
And left with some meaning spilt out from self.
When there is again a silence the heart shakes the body with noise.
Itself speaking. Testimony. As a lighthouse in viciously disinterested sea.

Then another silence. To have failed, so obviously. Speech tentatively
assertive, but with nothing clear to assert. The craft of singing
recruits apprentices from the abyss; from there it seems a bright profession
filled with gay colour. Deserts too are beautiful at a distance.
One cannot eat beauty. Song is no field to plough. It is a wildflower,
ploughmen scorn it. Colour is useless. A guild of dreamers
is no trade-union. To write ends in agony, always.
So this. Another silence. A voice in a bright labyrinth, a prison of colour.

Potato-land

for King Peter

Your family sleep in the palace
they are all dead but have been wound in
white cloth, glass cases

everything is impossible
or has been banned

a grey screen shows dictator and people
waving to each other, from balcony and street,
desperately, as though there were no language

The dinner hour

the lawns, of course, are of excellent stock,
the gardeners obedient & well qualified. everything
grows for them. the sky is of unmistakeable
craftsmanship, the trees wellchosen, the birds
of good character. a rustic bridge crosses the recirculated
stream. the distinguished poet and his
companions climb to an eminence and survey the gardens.
not for them the brothel cheer, the mystery of doorways.
they recline as though the hill were furniture.
from every part of the landscape
serpents glide silently toward them.
the birds watch, but do not forget to sing, nor the flowers
to smell sweetly, nor the white clouds to hasten to the
west. a great shadow walks into the lake,
chewing.

Philosophy of movement

the house stands by itself in the country.
the wind blows by itself. hills
a creek goes by quietly. birds rise,
a bright cloud, from the cool trees.
on the old slates, the sun tries to balance, rolls off,
falls among hills. the moon stands by itself.
cattle walk over a hill, their eyes connected, swivelling
toward a distance where the sun comes at night, from
treetop to treetop. walls stand, connected, yellow eyes
leaving the windows, black trees, bird ash, the existential moon.
time stands by itself: and from the landscape
cows, funiture and house depart.
stone, river, moon. treetops.
by themselves as if we had not come.

Surrexit dominus

all day we moved about, among unnecessary walls, each of us
cloistered in black...being useful, or praying, with the
detachment of clouds and the correct weight of involvement. each swam
in his own depths, swam, and drifted; drowning
was what happened at night. sometimes, though, night
was a month of black, a cowled season. hours of voices rising
beyond the husks of men became leaves in a mausoleum, moths
in a shale garden. the frozen poetry of psalms, chasms,
washed at us and eroded. i saw the mind as islands
whose sweet or acid tides would sometimes fall, leaving
the wrack of old ideas, some quicksand, and would show the land
to end like rotten teeth growing, decaying or would flood
over the useless barricades of faith. sunken ages' mute
spokesmen were eyes whose terrible reproaches gleamed from mute
depths. lastly, the sea became too haunted for them. gently,
they drifted away, into a fused midnight, and strong remained,
singing, walking on the water, the dead oceans.

In the park

they sit in the park, where it is green, where it is quiet
and green. a few hold their heads, some watch the tiny clouds, how they
fly. others have brought their sketchbooks; they draw the trees
singing, they draw each other and the clouds. they are here each day,
walking from the low buildings, returning with the moon and dream.
one, who is more adventurous, has entered the lake, where it is cool,
where it is green; she does not see the trees
or just their pale reflections where her face was.
her friends tow her to the shore, hair trailing in the water like a mermaid
they carry her home in state, she will be their queen.
the sketches are left on the grass, to be collected later
by a man with a pointed stick

e dead-weight of years crushing down, down,
gely destructive, yet has crushed from these barren lives
vine we'll call Australian, since no tariff has been paid.
ste it. Not bitter, but with the dust of the outback
ominent. Slide it around the palate. See with what rosy light
e chandelier blazes through this blood you suckle on.
nsider the delicate
uquet of revolution
was a good year for martyrs.
n Palach lit up half the silent east with his death agonies
ste the ashes you thought were sediment from long storage it is hard
forget. Remember too the vintners whose feet trod flat the grapes,
d flat the barbwire at Lone Pine so the press could sing,
g of 'significant advances', of selflessness. Taste it at V.C. Corner,
w many heroes then trod flat the fields to grow the grapes you think you
                                                          taste.
a amusing little vintage, you call it, vampires of humanity,
m your penthouse the world is beautiful the filth of streets is far below
e dead cannot be smelt unless the wind changes bringing you
e sound of death of city solitudes of labourers returning home exhausted
m factories you control. You suck their lives away, their spirit, an
                                                  amusing little wine.
ey toil that you can celebrate your profits, play aristo with some amusing
                                                                friends
awn from the endless ranks of profiteers, scuttling from Europe to get
                                          near the cash,
tting from Texas to pick up the pennies better men would scorn to touch.
was a good year, you say, the auditors agree; inside a wilderness a hermit
tens/the change he speaks of to the world will come; dare you face it?

Pioneer lane

Erskineville. The sun came round a corner,
and saw, and went. The sun's habitual corner.
Nothing unusual. The air they breathe
rolls out obscenely from the factory chimneys.
Old age. Just that. No more. And an appraisal
of work-years wasting in these sunless narrows
of terrace-streets which close themselves away,
rejecting newness like the baby stifled
by Leagues Club widows and the warm indifference
of public bars, and traffic loud and poisonous.
Day is so stale; sit in the sun; let it
warm away your questions. Things seem better
in the sun, even when you are old,
as old as these—or so we think—or almost.
Their retribution comes beyond the grave.
Not savage or pretentiously hostile,
they'll gather round, these veterans of Lone Pine
and Villers-Bret. and Passchendaele and Ypres,
a circle close with friendship; and there'll be
no pension-degradation; they'll be free,
these pioneers who made Australia
and fought to keep it, time on bitter time,
a place they could grow old in, never thinking
they'd be despised for even that senescence.
They think I know, of those who stayed behind
in the warm ridges of Gallipoli,
or Flanders mud. A cigarette-smoke circle,
two coins tossed high into the endless year,
falling to choruses of "Jesus Christ".

Journal d'un homme vide

my watch is slowing now that was
gold as stars in a child's
schoolbook, it slows and loses hours,
minutes blur, stretch, time dwindles
loosely, there is no form to it, no shape
but that of a flooded river which has lost
the sense of its banks. my blue watch. my green time.
last year the fashion was flowers   girls
wore watches with flower faces,
union jacks. the british flag
was in fashion three seasons and most
of a fourth: party walls
wore nothing but a flag, and plaster
for protection in the mornings. roads dwindle, too,
in the hills   we are soon rid of them, each other,
hours and the sun. in the end there is a fine zero,
nothing, the face, if you like, of the wind, a murderer
of leaves, cold friend of mountains. when the clock stops
it may go backwards, unreel the past.   or
merely be still, gather dust, learn sinecure ways.
be a holed, ancient teapot,
a blade with no handle, with an edge of victims

Differencias

Reality is superfluous
we have scrapped it
the replacement arrived today in a parcel from Asia
unpacking it we wondered how the community would react
forgetting that a rich society is not a community
forgetting that a rich society does not react.

We watch the moon dance
in its new blue raiment
have you not seen it?
or perhaps it was not televised,
perhaps the bosses could find no sponsor
nobody willing to underwrite so peaceful a revolution.

Oriental fumes; imagine brolgas and sea-horses, recall
in rising smoke the dawn at Moorabinda;
dreams measured in ounces worth more than Victorian gold
for these grew in the sun, grew wild, the sun, the gold fire
in the ocean,
in our heads

Arcangelo

more and more, of late, it becomes
difficult to be whole. the unity of self
is riddled through by doubt, which
devours concentration as small insects
might tunnel through a book seemingly
intact, but torn from certainty.
and there are interruptions. the sun
is torn from me by the wind of seasons changing,
merging, breaking. a branch rasps
against the window, voices of children

Lord, grant me one honesty. what I ask
is not the valour of being sure; perhaps
to hear again the wind, itself, a rivulet
flowing or falling; yes, even that, and know
it is divinity. But there is nothing
as positive. only
from time to time
when there is no-one near
comes a small sound, as a child's voice,
which i take and pass on to reed and string,
hoping for the one
note to appear, and be
wind on high stone, or a river; hoping
somehow to please You with my song

Vespers

harpsichord evening sallow west children
ginger cat treehigh clouddown
fragility of too few dimensions
rococo
gems and purple thoughts of Tasso
monastic in an imaginary cave
the wind the silence the inconsequences

sordid hours too slow in passing
excesses dwindle still too much of night
inoperable cancer of the soul

brick garden iron flowers plastic Apostles
obsolescence of virtue
what do they give us in exchange for peace?
neither simplicity nor execution.

as in a photograph, how
nothing will change, and how the mildew
eats immortality

The card game *(a narrative)*

She loved him, you see,
and he another.

Lacking the courage to propose,
she devised a communication.
Being (I suppose) a symbolist of sorts,
she sent him a card;
the two of hearts.
He replied with the Joker.
Distraught, she, thumbing through the
pasteboard things,

encountered the
Ace of Spades,
took appropriate action.

He, callous knave,
did not see fit
to follow suit.

Afternoon

for Rodney Hall

climbed
to the top
saw
there was no higher
I could go
and seeing fell
so far
so high
Tower of Babel
Babylon
the hanging

Hangover

learning to walk again, and fly,
and shouldering the crucifix
of one's stupidity

tentative morning—one
limps in and out of luck,
of too-late wisdom / shutting stable doors
before the poem goes, a Yesenin
horse the rarest shade of pink

among the ruins, what we save,
to tread among them,
gingerly, afraid of breaking,
is painful pleasure, like first days at school.

W.F. Bach

this music tells me
more than headlines and history

creativity
a forgotten habit
had woken in time

in time

all forward and backward
movement halts while
you write a dialogue for flute and oboe

all the kings horses

Going away

shoes, ties, handkerchiefs, odd details to remember
at such a moment. Leaving the for last time
on the long voyage into solitude.
The past floods round, and there is no escaping
memories, big as icebergs part-submerged
but floating into horrid consciousness.
The past, the future, they are one, the present
an agony of huge apostasizing
of all one's life till now. Packing to go,
taking love's seasons in a dusty suitcase
out through the sky and through a hundred days
which will be purgatory intensified.
What will be left after another love
has grown and gone and faded into diaries
filled with the glad oblivion removing
sequences from realities and from
illusionary roles we call existence?

Duet

Worn
gramophone record of my days;
today I took a ticket
in the Vietnam lottery
unlikely they'll conscript me
there have been enough soldier poets;
yesterday we spent
a fortune of love
on Mona Vale Beach
amused ourselves deftly kissing
I lost my tongue writing a ballad
on the warm tissues inside your mouth
held your heartbeat in my hands
outside our faces your tortoiseshell
hair striated the sun;
we fit together well you said
an ivory puzzle of bones
comfortable pastime of limbs;
in winter's ballet
love depends on choreography of chance
and poetry is breathless
words to each other
scarce heard for kisses and the rowdy surf.

Notes for an inquest

Ten oclock
the bells of the city
a blonde girl
blue shirt and blue eyes
there are gardens of her
no-one will know how
in her sea eyes
virginity is a permanence.
Cocaine appetites are starvation
I burn for it, the white
powder of death and paradise and pleasure.
Waiting on a cold stone
corner for the connection.
It is late
it will be much too late
death follows me
a naked rider on a ravaged horse
grey clouds descend
I am drowning
unable to swim in air any longer
or tread water through the solitary
abyss of deprivations.
These people are agonies
their eyes beseech Him but the thumb is down
there must be a kill;
I am the sacrifice they are expecting
day lessens and diminishes
to two points of light which,
even now, còuld be mistaken for eyes.
Merciless vicars of abstinence
repeal me I am free now I am
disenfranchised
my fate is my own

my redemption also
what must I do
what shall I choose?
The clock advances
a sentinel questions me
name, rank, religion?
I have none. I am this hand
pushing a pen along
in random patterns
my fate is my own
I have nothing to say to them
or to their questions;
the question I would answer but cannot
was in her eyes.
So I wait, alone, expiating;
a greyness among grey,
weak among stone.
I will be the first to break.
My hands tremble the pen falls;
who to retrieve it?
Desolation is a drughungry morning
moving along the sick and hopeless paths
towards a bitter afternoon. Defeat.

Studio

reality crowds you
your eyes are full of circumstance
a place a season a hallucination

you see what is before you
nothing else
the present is too present

so art becomes environment
and so environment is art
the eye filled with its history of sight

what you create is what you see
and soon see only what you've made
your diary is to look around.

Partita

I am living alone now
contained in one small room
the walls cry with rats' cries
the window rejects me like a mirror
winter suspends.

It is necessary that I perform a catharsis:
I require this of myself;
to void the mind utterly,
leaving no clues behind, nothing
on which to base a philosophy.

The past is strangely tangible,
I would rid myself of it.
I have no plans. Only
to exit from the body, and fly
through the white rain of summer

the dance showed no uncertainty
of step. something moving
exquisitely. doubt. blindness.
we are all weeping. there has been
another death. how
shall we dance in marble.
restrictions. hallucinations, certainty,
induced by very strange
acts. what does the eye accept,
and what reject, of seeing?
drowned in exquisiteness
we shall have danced
so lightly, almost
carelessly, through
years of unbearable recurrence.
a movement in green,
light, agony
becoming art, and art,
protracted suicide.

First Casino poem

The piano
like Monk or Bogart
insistently
part of the scene
is inseparable from the mood.

Tuesday night
in the colonies—
we go to draw on the rum ration
or smoke a hoarded pipe of opium
... lost like Rimbaud.

The meaning
does not matter
really
to us
veterans of a
seasonal campaign,
and the music
even as the wind
or a river
ends so soon we are aghast
at being unprepared.
Piano
ivory and ebony
like a terribly intricate
and lovely chess war.

Bill Evans Trio
jazz for believers
a gospel like
smoke or like empty lanes
with, in a thistle-poor field,

a black horse, a white,
old companions in the tongueless wisdom of age,
for summers on the island of
five hundred miles from her.

The notes of another tune
accustom me to them and then are gone
inadvertant like an ephemeral
butterfly.

It it time yet
to dream in the ether-drowsiness
distant from desire?

Like moth to taper
I return to the lyric
resignation of theories too mythological.
These are reality.

I am the merchant of the Muses now,
selling my stanzas door to door
among the cognoscenti.
Complex bitternesses
ubiquitous as clouds
are tasted among all the fragrances.

Night is a
burden for the wakeful . . . shall we call it
insomnia or inspiration or madness?

Unexpected fluency
lets me sing
late into Tuesday.

Wednesday, not yet on the horizon,
reminds me of a penthouse, of a
past friend. Where do they go?
from vision to distant lands, to
coasts and palm oases in the shifting
dunes of contemporary history.

Faces
are simpler than
names

I have no preference.

Hallucinogens and lovers.

Finally, the body breaks down.
Exhaustion, problems of imparting;
agonies of a personal nature.

What does one do
to end it?
An overdose? Of what?

Swinburne felt this way,
died for fifty years
in a tall house in England.

Sheer physical
revulsion at any activity ...
no discriminations exercised any more,
just
waiting for the show to finish.

Brooke's formula or Sassoon's
for immortality

is not relevant to civilians—
we linger in the half-light
and may not speak, not sing.

All the poets of Ecclesiastes and Howl and the voices
of Memnon or of Delphi
have gone beyond the high clouds
over the narrow mountain pass.
Few are known now,
few remembered.

I waste
without motive
my tomorrows
never come
and today
is inconceivable.

Parables of the sacred fools, of
Basho and Ryokan and Corbiere,
do not apply,
for they were sacred
I
must find my way
alone to the
green pastures
the quiet waters of David.

dear charles: it is dreadful here. i should not have come. the
people are like draped statuary, they *feel* nothing. their city
is glass, but nothing breaks or marks it. i walk among these
dummies, and they appear to walk, also, and make voices. nothing
lives here. last night i dremt of your city. i heard a girl
weeping, high, perhaps at a window; looking up, i saw nothing,
nothing, and when i woke a raven sat regarding me. white bulbous
clouds massed at its head. i think constantly of death. the room
seems smaller than when i arrived: doors are terrible, charles,
they. . . the handwriting becomes illegible, the nib has
torn the page here; no more is discernible. silent crowds ebb
past the windows; a slow procession, without flags; no
singing. a lemon burns on the table, or is wax; light bursts up from
empty candlesticks, falters, dies. in the dark air
a movement, as of wings

to Charles Buckmaster

Studio IV

But to have been there
fragile in an eggshell of illusions
was more than inescapably
to have a past

Waking early, cold and because
the wooden walls admitted dawn
and chooks outside announced the Coming
hours before morning had arrived.

It would be Sunday
chill dim abstracts
from airwaves you'd discern
Aldeburgh music or a fairytale

Involved in that, huddled in too few blankets
you had no chance to notice how the sun
thawed violence, how a free and peaceful moment
was overrun by day and you by horror.

what's left of you is not enough
to hold a mind together or,
except in one bright image, make
a literature of all this pain

you build a fire the shadows arch
around you just above the flames
and as the yellow meal of warmth
cinders, a rushing silence numbly eats you.

A living corpse is what they find,
stick figure, saturated puppet;

they can devise no use for you
whom life rejected years ago

so thin—a single room somewhere
anchored to being by a cable
woven to all that you desired
the tiny worlds you.cherish and which own you

Life's walking-wounded come to see
this new mutation of despair
and solitude is not allowed
but sorrow and this dusty sense of waiting

Becoming sky

he takes for ingredients the purity of the moon,
a fall of rain and sunlight, streets of chance people.
he mixes them well, he will drink them like the night.

charade: the wind brushes his hair, he sits in a window,
waiting for clouds or angels. comicbook figures
distract him. he goes outside, through the pale
curtains of forethought.

the bottles weigh his coat: he appears old,
a secondhand character. gissing and dostoevsky
abandon him to an oblivion of torn paper.

up between buildings the sun is exchanged
for the moon. stars come or go; there are clouds
and for a friend, the rain. it washes his exhaustion,
and the pavement: he will sleep in a clean place
and wake up with pneumonia.

Illness

in bed with the unknowable, in irreconcilable,
legs and arms cut off by pain, missing;
days clot, go hard on me, rigid with
difficulties. my bed as uncomfortable as a
shelf of books, to lie on

the lady of shalott, i set mirrors to make a world
inside. so trees fill my room, there is a chimney
in one corner, by the table of sickroom flowers.
a black bird flies in the window, clouds massed at its head;
regards me, chief of a white realm from which
threads dangle

food is brought; it steams for a while, then flies gather,
pick at it. i sleep; my cat senses a danger in the black bird,
makes it to vanish. the cat hunts for a bright cure; later,
i wake to a caught mouse grey and small and dead on the pillow.

Chaconne for a solipsist

The most significant fact about this room is that nothing
else exists. Beyond the walls, nothing. Space, perhaps,
infinite and invisible. The windows are mirrors. Why
look out when one can look in? There is no furniture.
It is more amusing to imagine new, different furnishings
each day, than to wake to the same shapes, colours,
textures, polish. Today, next year, yesterday, it is one.
On a wall—or is it the floor—is a clock I built once,
or shall build, or am building. Its two hands are identical, so one may never decipher their mute semaphore.
Opposite, a pool of green, blue, or colourless, liquid,
sometimes reflects and sometimes invents. I think of this
room as a filing cabinet, a memory bank where the
history of fantasy is stored. The fantasy of history.
Dreams are sculptures, names are poems, nobody comes
for there is no-one else, and nowhere from which to
come. I am Proust, de Vigny, Owen Aherne, myself—
the identities are interchangeable. The mind is an
entertainment, a circus where philosophers perform.
I inhabit the drawing room Rimbaud imagined at the
bottom of a lake, purple tincture of opium. An indent-
ical self represents me in the salons of my friends on the
previous planet, they will not notice I have gone.
Everything is imaginary, everyone; only caprices,
masquerading as ideas, populate the air. It is difficult
sometimes for me to remember that I too am imaginary.
The world has neither ended nor begun, but I may
occupy myself believing that it exists. I could no more
create it than it could create me; central consciousness
is the only force neither positive nor negative. It must
be a giant joke gone awry, a lysergic acid rave, Robinson
Crusoe on the wrong island. But still an island, bounded

35

by seas I shall never sail. Solitudes. Pacing impatiently
the cage of body, of self. An exit glitters brightly in
my hand.

Platform 16, Central Station

Disembodied. This is not I. Yet
to be somehow a part of this. Gray
smoke is all the air, a tin awning the sky,
the ground concrete. Trains shunt by
noisily, but there is no sound. That left
an hour ago, tomorrow it may be in Brisbane,
far north of these delusive afternoons.
Here love is like the east wind, the ocean wind
coming every second month, when it comes
and has sung and gone away it will seem unreal.
So with life. Coming and going, rarely
to destinations we anticipated.
Strangers drift by, gulls in railway uniform
passing to other shores of night than this.
A transitory world, trains and people both,
the ugly landscape our memorial;
platform 16, Central Station.

The Barcoo rot

Wary of melodrama
I'd quietly gone

on an occasionally
streetlit voyage

away, far, past burnt
Drayton, the wine hills

and Hunter stone
and to the thirsty Moonbi Ranges

there is nothing
one cannot endure

extremes
are tolerable

even, now, desolate,
peering from exhaustion

toward defeat, I am serene —
one could suffer more

the face as travellers' faces are—
weathered, expressionless, not without humour.

Desert fragment

As they came nearer, they saw that the house had been dead
a long time. There was no glass in the windows, and walls which
from a distance had appeared solid were seen to be loose brick
held together by a tapestry of weeds. It was a small
ruin, standing alone and barely visible from the track.
Here, on this plain, the gold rush had faltered, died.
Survivors drifted back to the towns, leaving untidy
mounds of mullock, windlasses over dry shafts,
wooden crosses where now the crows sat, their expressions
varying little between bored and baleful. It was as though a pocket
of death had begun to grow, past the derelict pubs and the ruinous grail
of a horse-trough, to the railed grave of three tourists who had
died of exposure after their sedan broke down.
The last tenant of the house was an old man who came from the big
smoke tired, disillusioned. In this land the old had nothing but
memories and an inadequate pension. . .

Lonely as a cloud

The end is distance. A day
too great. You are surpassed. Your steps cannot be equated
with such immensity. You sit on the track,
waiting. You do not ask yourself
why you wait — exhaustion is its own answer
and there could be
no justification of all this silence. A single tree
shades you from noon. It is as though
you have achieved some irredeemable
godhead; as if all your life you have striven
for this isolation. Detail distracts you:
even out here, crows live — their black
drift through enormity. Ants. Beetles. Grass.
You cut across a paddock, thinking to save
some miles. They will find first your swag, then
your clothes abandoned.
The cities have a more subtle way of death. How white
your skeleton will be, naked,
picked clean, in the next summer's
furnace solitude. How marvellously simple — the white
bones, the orange grainy texture of the plains, blue millennia.
You are pleased by the stylisation of your death.
The crows, too, express interest; also the ants.

Memoirs

One redbilled waterhen forms a quiet raft
on the slow river. Casuarinas dwindle
into the broad proportions of the sky.
We are voices in air
feet on a path
scarcely perceptible. Bubbles rise
where an eel, all but hidden,
rests in the slime below the bank.
Bitterness becomes a habit
persistent like Sisyphus,
our hopes outrun us. If we sank in the water
only ripples would survive. Like smoke from
crematorium chimneys. Like speeches
left by a murdered statesman. Like our poems.
We drive away, though, in the old car,
it holds so many months of disillusion
the sky falls down and covers us with clouds
grayer than ashes and too sad to breathe.

Salix

growing isn't in proportion
when we leave the past behind
all of us grows except our eyes
and simple things like faith and love

the games the adults play are new
for a while, yes, and maturity
equips us with seven-league boots
but nowhere to go

so bitterness, so cynicism;
age gives, at worst, nostalgia,
at best, serenity, or sleep—
childhood leaves no survivors.

Birch trees, Courland Penders

days of birches white grey black
skies moving are lilyponds
the wind describes itself to elms

stonewall parkland forestyellow
ages of stone ages of green
nature a series of deaths

upright house toppling into colours
grey as the skin of phantom
drifting and fading

life becomes the dance of hours
whose ideal would be moments
seconds instants particles

of light when the rain falls
merging into volcanic
skin of the last bright season

The Duke of Courland his pavan

there are days when
the sun exists for us in roomfuls

we feel a finely
executed change in latitude
and all our rituals
so familiar
produce unsummoned
forces, surprised to be remembered,
baleful, or rubbing their eyes
at so little
change since the days of Abelard

swifter and louder, these, more populous,
but sour, meaningless . . . a backstreet world

Song

She dances in the colours I see
colours I paint with my eyes
she moves like something artists would paint
sun in a sky/blue and lemon
O and how the sky changed with her smile
and the colours were much too close
So I watch morning turn into a dream
tapestried on wind and waters
Look we are in the park, lost as leaves
seen through a hollow face

birdcall and branches heavy with fruit
spill on the shadowy pathway
leading us nowhere

clouds fall and cover us with sky
we drown in light, the shore too far now
truth is less than what we see
lies that the dead have left in stone
may be the prison they take us to
in their frightened town

when love is flowers turning to stone
we shall not walk here again
love is the sun to me, and the flowers
die where there is no sun
dream of a land where love
will be like a flower once more
dream that we are the sun

(Sung to the Spanish Dance No. 10 "The Oriental" by Granados
played on lute, harp or guitar.)

Richmond River

These northern towns look better from a distance,
lurking at road's end, innocent as postcards.
Nimbin crouches upland in the green
backyard of a banana plantation, guarded by stone giants.
Casino, outpost of the eighteen fifties,
waits for a death which has already come.
Glass-fronted firetraps in the meagre streets
array infinities of dusty wares;
greek and dutchman swill in brick hotels—
we'd missed the drovers by a hundred years.

But the insects. Wasp flights raiding with dust,
cockroaches in the council.
Only, sometimes, to meet Australia, to have visions
cities can't provide, compensated.
On the beach at Ballina, though, we found the natives friendly.
Their bright bikinis melted, expendable, and after,
warm in their brown sea-tasting bodies,
we found a better pastime than exploring.

The sun but not our children

west of the inland edge
some odd survivals

these are
what is left
of a subjective
history

the Innamincka bottleheap
the Tibooburra willow

where Sturt came through
a cairn was raised
where Burke died
they fenced off a coolibah

the air, museum dry, preserves memorials
the sun but not our children will have honoured

Chopin: the winter wind

Sad fluency
begins as the black
treading of pallbearers.
The storm has not yet broken
but today I found
a sparrow frozen into
almost sculptured death.
Then, the sudden
immediacy of the fourth season,
the threat of treetops shaken,
windchime of frostsilver branches,
waves against stone, a coach-ride,
the view through misted panes
of a pale forest; and a paler,
vision-thin man,
his hands busy with nets of black
figures, the future of music.
Nohant Mallorca Paris Zelazowa
genius recounts this saga
in an austerity of years and chords,
a lyricism perfected by suffering
transposed upward into
triumphs of form the mind hears longest.

Sickroom

the room distils me
through what I reject

its walls and spaces gather me
among what I have gathered

my books and shells
my violin and rifle

tenants of a spider's lair
dull in a sick man's candlesight

symbols of where steps led
and led away from

Island farm

rooms hang above the city
are exposed to light dark wind
rain & other visitors

in a shop
cages hang
among other cages
in a wall of caged birds

these too
know light and dark

in the city
we are allowed to walk
we may jump up fall down turn a somersault
eat or not eat

we vote for faces on television
for names in the press
one year we glimpsed the queen's white glove
which waved to us

five hundred miles along the coast
my farm grows
the sheep fatten the trees bear fruit
wildbirds come for the crops

unattended it lives
without voting or pretending

lying ill
in a cliff room

among other rooms in cliffs
i think beyond the city

to the farm and sea

things become larger as we leave
and distance magnifies

The harvest is past, the summer is ended, and we are not saved
                                        —Jeremiah 8,20
Be astonished, O ye heavens, at this, and be horribly afraid, be
very desolate . . . for my people have committed two evils;
they have forsaken me the fountain of living waters, and hewed
them out cisterns, broken cisterns, that can hold no water.
                                        —Jeremiah 2, 12—13

Making a chapel
it is best
not to expect too much

what comes
in answer
to your rites
may be no more
than disillusion

the temple of leaves
lit by the moon
when winter came
there were no leaves
the moon was a grey stranger

the temple of carved stones
stood high among the winds
which blew it down
and rain erased what it
had tried to say

truly
I think
the best temple
will have been
within the skull
a white place

lit by the eyes which left no ash
sung by the lips
that left no mark
upon the stone
of those who came

among the seasons
comes unexpectedly
a day without gravity

your arms float above your head
clothes move freely, as slow
branches in a storm

you rise, seeing a field
a landscape, an atlas page
rounding away below

white flowers

all your possessions follow you
sailing in loose formation

this is what death is
the food in sealed urns
the sacrificed attendants

you crash into the moon
spilling white limbs in the pale
suspension

in conscious orbit
round the great mind
bored/trapped/imperishable

Astalot

geometry of waking, surfacing
among the remnants of hallucinations

all that you left around you of last night
finds an occasion to remit perception

gives back its colour to the eye, its shape
and texture to the hand, its taste to mouth

morning's dimensions seem approachable
if you rise gently, almost wearily

from where the visions left you, filled with mirrors
towards inconstant images and dreams

rise gently
when the moon becomes a flower

for if the mirrors broke, their shattering
might wake what you have only guessed and dreaded

Stalin-style

when the train stops they are in a grey
siding of night/
the wind is voices rising, falling,
fading. some of the people sleep/
the children play in their time.
an old man tells them
night, the merlin with a cloak, stars
silverpainted on it.
the train moves again, jolting to
terrible destinations. day opens the
eyes of huddled sleepers. is the sun through
ribs, glorious, NOTHING, shining
like gold in shattered mouths

Sitting on a fortune

the scene, some sort of
morning, coldwater
flat off Dixon Street
someone had left a girl behind
she gropes for waking
her eyes have broken
fragments of blue and green
what worlds they have contained
and swept away, Haymarket
Magdalen. her arms resemble
nailholes or nickelmines.
the school she left to come here
would have taught her useless lessons
she prefers to chance it in orange
vortex of shot, the white powder of vision. need, not pleasure,
pipes her down midnight lanes to make
the curious for twenty dollars each
translating the smokeblown
unfoldings of herself, warm
givings and taking, into the rent and breakfast,
horse and snow. fifteen years have taught her
cities of twenty dollar streets
a bluejean spacewalk through the jealous
sunday paper hypocrites
who know the ways to profit
but have lost the right to speak

The face in the mirror

music drowns out the traffic.
he leans against a wall. has closed his eyes.
barters the contents of his mind
for contents of a hypo. is the gigolo of a
thousand bored readers at a dollar a time.
someone kicks the wall over & he falls
flat.

Camelot lane

indiscriminate survivals
the best go first the mediocre last
it is the same to sun and moon
they see beyond the individual
to constellations lit by burning
brothers of the star tribe

we, in our streets, our enclaves,
caught up in living
cannot conceive these vast
forces we speak the words wither
we write the ink runs out
we move our doubles mock us / to continue
this game of continuity / imperfections,
imperfections, imperfections.

destroy yourself or live forever it is
the same action imperfect always nothing
will change this faulty incarnation
neither to die nor break is change
to be the same a lecher or a priest
is always us. Only, once,
hearing a creek fall far into a gorge
that seemed a separate world, and trees and bellbirds
and nobody for miles, had been content.
For several minutes.

Symptoms

Only reality tastes unfamiliar.
Disoriented, a mariner dismasted
in an unknown sea, without a landfall,
I return within myself to grasp at any certainty. Sureness carries an expire
guarantee. But I inhabit these illusions
as one would a great forest.
They are comfortable. They are all I recognise.
Being constantly lost among neon
sculptures, assaulted by concrete,
one learns to take precautions.
The mind malfunctions, it goes on strike for better conditions,
better dreams. Dreams are like women:
ignore them, and they surround you.
Pursue, and they are gone. Can one believe them?
Claustrophobia heads my check-list of extremes;
a little town shrank in like an unwilling cave,
the city follows me everywhere.
I search for green islands, Romanticism,
for human dignity, in a world that offers us
temporary lodgings.

When her last poems

when her last poems appeared,
posthumously, columnists babbled
of 'outstanding', 'spirited',
spoke of qualities, deathbed virtuosity.
as if it mattered. saw that she was of air,
called her butterfly who had flown
higher than eagles.
as if her death meant nothing.
(coffins having no windows)

height above height it rises, music
blind as a mountain
the almost ceaseless climb, scaling
emotions, colours, distances
grey as a peacock and as gloriously
careless of all else but beauty .
he is no fool who would forsake the
government of fools
for the long forest vigil and above
the world and wilderness his
tower of gods oceans surpassing form

Death as triumph

the final years were worst. Loosely existing,
preserving his identity through friends,
'the poet as the letter X', resisting
all but the past because that never ends.
He seemed to build a labyrinth consisting
of everything he loved, that distance rends
and passion clouds with fateful nearness, misting
clear sight with the depths that sight extends

The High were fair—they left him eyes that close,
and senses to forbid the scented rose,
seductive art that steals the mind from time
for love of symphony, for love of rhyme,
a hand that, trembling, knew to use the blade
of self-excision, finding Self unmade.

Hands

they are like sparrows, her small
hands, darting about, making empty
gestures in the air
when she touches the keyboard
notes drop like insects at the end of autumn

his nervous hands dangle, nothing to
hold, reach for someone who passes,
who does not stop, and the claws return
with a thread caught in them

she sits bulkily on a dwarfed
chair, and in the sweating
hugeness of her fingers,
even a goblet disappears

they stand in a corner
they think they are in love
many drinks have drained into them
she leans on a wall as he caresses her
his hands as busy as maggots on a dead bird

the host, with his
remora wife,
shakes hands with their departing guests.
he is neither large nor old.
his handshake leaves an impression of both.
dry weightless touching
as the wind would feel
in curtains of loose skin

July the nineteenth, 1969

for Wendy Morrow

Suburban winter weekend's day; wake late,
outside no morning heralds you with sunlight.
From a construction site, saws and hammering;
traffic on asphalt avenues, the sun,
mere disc of almost-white, so insubstantial.
The garden makes its own decisions now
about survival and the length of branches.
The pines are taller and the gums have grown
faster than love would, stronger than a promise.
The bottlebrush afire, the daphne out,
a decadence of flowers, different birds
holding their conversation in a maple.
Grey except these, the day proceeds immeasurably;
I hear the sound of weeping from next door.

'I want my paintings to be comfortable armchairs'

—Matisse

been a bit sick lately, & sick of
great art dispassionately moving, moving by, saying
everything sayable, rephrasing cliches, & whole
great slabs of monotonous observation, ragbags
to hold the junk that swirls round genius' head. when
people are civilised, the world ordered, nobody freaked, its
time enough for the faceless disembodied *comfortable*
cliches to crawl out like maggots from a
prison meal & sort of sneer at you, for neat
duodecimo's full of abstraction. but now
they are burning the live & dead, in vietnam,
in money wars, & kittens like foetuses flushed down society's
toilets—have you seen a baby die, any of you,
do you know about grief? its
so personal, so tiny and huge a state,
that it is all you know, & there's
no art but life then, & you grow a bit
tired of shakespeare beethoven bach freud
aeschylus goethe dante etc etc etc etc etc

Poem for charlie

Dispossession; inside
each season as though hollow
you grow and are a part of nothing,
everything. Apart. Especially, in extreme
times, to have nothing.
Belonging nowhere, all this
the outside of some high
philosophy. Indefinite—
having learned that
a definition is an epitaph
—you move like sunlight
inside each moment's universe.
As though a girl had kissed you, and you'd woken
from human sleep, and found the bridge and crossed it,
and were no part of this umbrella city,
no part of what they term 'reality'.

for Charles Buckmaster

To a lover going

Finally the world
seen through too many bottles
is not rosy not bloodred
but this opaque deathless death of wishing
all the doors have been closed
I've said goodbye to
what remained of anything that
might have mattered to me once
all else is either debris or superfluous
or will turn bad when morning makes
its hollow ringing on the shutters
so leave the taste of warmth awhile
and turn the light out when you go

For Charles Blackman

by itself on
a grey embankment
with handfuls of grass
the telephone box
is very red.
presently while a
black kitten stalks
mysteriously through
hill weeds
a girl comes
in a blue dress.
the shape of
her legs in
black stockings
excels the sky.
she talks to
someone distant
perhaps
who has a white yacht
and takes her
often
on the green harbour
the wind filling
sails and her clothes
with the same
impulse.

The Cocklebiddy fisherman

for Tom Shapcott

His net is dadaist
he fishes silence
the heat   this almost
living desolation
meridian of sand   what
trips the mind could take
not limited by desert or by scorn.

As gentle as a Queensland poet, he
rows on the Nullarbor in an open boat
redpainted like those other
ochred hunters.
He'll share his meal of
tea and munga with you,
lend his oasis world to tourists' children

but if you touch him
will he be mirage?

Small

watching the ants,
making a road through the sand to
help them. watching clouds what they become.
holding court in a circle of
grave dolls.
under the leaves it never rains.
spider pie for tea.

Cafe society

sitting at round
footpath tables
the civilised
watch from their coffee
from a smokescreen of detachment
selecting victims
from acquaintances

like the carrion eaters
of the desert
each one
picks at delicacies
the eyes
the genitals
the soul

we see them feed
on what they have despoiled

at other tables
their prey
do likewise
then lick their talons and depart

home in their careful studios
the wives watch
helpless petals
one by one
fall from the plastic flowers

Arcangelo

where the hill falls tidal
grasses begin a shore
birds like salt lift or float

arms and legs stretch beyond sight
across the sand
and wings in the sea's immediacy
and voices along the edges of direction

something has landed

not of the sea
nor from the reeds'
refracted green

an impression of others

tangible summer clouds'
          white
          landscape

invisible companions gather
who speak when the wind speaks
who robe themselves with the sea

the edges of direction   a coast
        immediacy

salt birds lift   high   above the shore
the sea and land retreat
        enormous sun
        whose shadow i call distance
        because it vanishes

In the high country

crossing the mountains, a bare,
vestigial track spiders up scree slopes,
shale falls. we watch the valley rise into blue,
perfect voids. the wind sweeps low the trees,
we spin prayer wheels, think of the meal
miles ahead. the path zigzags up; three solitary climbers
inch higher. one above the other, another
unseen above him; repeated; poplars in a
rain pond

but now the path
climbs sharply, and those who would continue
breathe, think and breathe again.

old men's feet make
promises
on midnight roads

The dry

meagreness evaporates
the billabong ebbs
into the sky its beauty
a net of mudcracks

herons and tribes
go walkabout
to a district of
trustier waters

stock and ambition die
the dusty blue of summer

Before the hour of streetlights

his afternoon is
orange at moments
and sometimes pale

shadow walks
across the floor
as slow as morning

the wind falls
a violin

at the window
barely moving
petals of rose

the day is
his supreme work
the artist of slight movement

the composer of
almost
stillness

the poet
who
senses

at the window
the yellow
butterfly of death

The grandfather

for J.M.S.

inside the gates his drive is a chain of ponds. the car stalls,
we walk the rest of the way. arriving at his verandah
we are met by green relatives, scented, waving, touching us.
he pushes the door, which falls open; no-one and footsteps.

the land he holds is time's reward. bare, wily trees take over,
cling for a living to the stone, and orchids
wild in an echo stable.

he tells the story of the ghost; we dine; outside, the wind
catches the high, rusted sails of a windmill which cries
red dust in dimming air. crows rise from a roof, it is time to go.

back in the city, the middle of a week, none of him
seems real. the house, thousands of acres gone to seed, would be
his flying ship which turned to stone, a girl
he visits instead of dying, his Dutchman's port of call.

if life were love, and grew no more from
greed, hatred, leavings of departed
gods, we should be a little less
inclined to search. & if the strange
bread of a roadside brotherhood cd be
fed to them in the towns, & they wd
drink from the skies and not of
the wares of Bacchus or the Water Board.
if they. if we. if.

easy to leave, tho easier to stay.
we go. beyond their places, in
easier & harder air, washed &
eaten by the weather, we can
examine principles. here, are we
anywhere? the emptiness could
blunt an axe.
nowhere. nothing. dust
and the word of strangers.

merely to depart
is no answer.
freedom's not in evasion. but to search
horizons for their meaning, and to meet
with rainclean eyes
whatever faces you
when distance ends

To the colour red

not in the commerce of the day,
although it is complete and done well,
and pleases him; nor in walking
from market to his house
along the river; not just his eye,
how it will circle about something
and capture, not the thing, but its
essence; nor in his cooking, which
pleases him; at night, in the morning,
on spare days, while he mixes his colours
deftly, takes up a brush he's made
from the tail of his daughter's pony
and a twig from the garden, his other
world opens, he is able to tell,
to share; he will take you riding
in the red orchard and the blue
perfection of a forest he has dremt;
the complete man; because he does not
ruin it in doubts.

the day veers from its track, needs some adjustment,
something is wrong which must be sensed
rather than observed. the controls have slipped.
the motel floor is mopped dry, it seems
better, the glass swept away with sunshine and
deosited in a container of sharp, glittering days.
he sits on the roof, designing the perfect
invulnerability of movements. he sits on the roof,
designing the perfect
invulnerability.

the ground is fragile with snow, the controls have
frozen. technicians come from town, fix everything,
fix everyone. with a blowtorch they heat whats wrong,
with a microscope they highlight the great fault of
inevitabilities. he knows the word for it, he sits on
the floor, head between knees, he knows the word they
call it by.

the dark and powerful cars are parked in the drive but under the
black paint they are ready, a key would wake them.
a key would start them on their way. although she is
wrapped in a carpet her feet protrude, perhaps they are not dead.
still she is smiling. she wanted none of this. there is no escape.

Presences

at last the night comes, stifling the sun
with horizons, a hangman's drop,
steps for the thirteen hours of today. above the roofs something
like a bitten eye races the bombers home, to their
black fields and iron houses. uneasily
some stars come, our jewelled neighbours, cold
as a distance, as a loss. the other side of darkness
is where she lives, the
land and sea and land away.
her kiss is a postmark and her voice
sounds along wire. we meet
on week-old pages like cliches. but
around her bed and mine, I know the same
winter steals, which chills the body and makes
air a frozen moat, and objects islands, and
which is not winter.

Abdication

THERE ARE MORNINGS WHEN THE
sun exists for us in roomfuls, and
night a hallway at a time, and even the
world has been reduced to an autumn homestead
in a no longer certain landscape. we have reorganised
the system of agriculture and now our miles of country
graze not cattle but clouds and rather than supervise the
mending of fences i walk among old errors of commission
the world lessens the war keeps its distance and the moon respects our exi‍

Bum's rush II. Through the ice

Time stops. Thats the first sign. And you wait.
Nothing more happens. You are left alone
with no surprises to anticipate.
The air becomes lead and your heart inert, like a stone
figure in some forgotten gallery.
Endlessness traps you, a maze of frustrating limits, a flaw
in the seeming perfection of the six-day blueprint that failed. Sea
and sky refuse you automatically, you are no freer than before.

Across morning

for Hilary

Areas

the light at the window
grey, seeming to petrify
the world outside, the world
inside, the world of
glass itself. there are
hungers of foodlessness, of
sleeplessness, hungering
after righteousness and
just lately
we are discovering
other starvations

Across Morning

across morning
the kitten walks about
in the enormous room, in the
rubble of our life. like an eye
she moves through collections, stands
on our clothes, on discarded things, and now
watches us like a mirror.

she has thrust into the uncommon, the
private exquisitenesses, where being
is a candle in a cold room,
is an empty cup, a row of
books like stones. in the bedroom
our public faces point at one another, baffled,
baffled.

Still Life

afterwards   wine   pretences   and
sight   honey   fall   answers
finds   bread   as   meet
its way   and   leaves   the
to   sunlight   whose   mirror
a   on   autumn
stiller   a   comes
subject   table

Third seer's tale

left to his own   mainly literary   devices
the prince of the moon spun at late hours
no rhetoric   nor longish narratives
Sang most often of the sky   what he knew
of it His songs were printed and distributed
as by the wind   he was soon famous   The prince
of the moon knew three ladies His mother
who was the sun   His sister
the queen of spades   wed
to the king of deepest space   And his lady
the star ariel   Her brother
rigel sought duel   but was thwarted   quicksilver
His seven houses of the moon knew love   his
Knew also balladeers wizards itinerants debt collectors
The song of the prince of the moon is too long
to be sung   Outlasting voices   mercury
grew deaf from overhearing   venus
cold shouldered him   bored   and saturn
cast up deadly spells   The prince
employed three seers One asked for silver
and was beheaded   One asked for nothing/ascetic
starved   The third
decamped with ariel
The moon sings best of astral bodies   knew nothing
of love   the seer left him a fine stone
castle   true   and portraits on the back of cards

Falling asleep in snow

distances leave you first
drained from the eyes
vision is interrupted
close objects vanish into white
you shield the eyes from disappearances

inside is memory
flickering like the forgery of lamplight
when all you have is this
you do not flinch from going back
into the silent, scarcely real, land

the wind in frozen things no longer rustling
you fade, sink, lose yourself
in numbness. in enormity.
falling asleep in snow, in drifts of
fictioned memory

you are porous now, and absorb
all that has been outside,
years, cold, and weather
and drown where crushed white enters
through the punctures in yr arms

Journal d'un homme vide

Three Aprils ago the road was the best escape, the sea beyond the
road might have been a moat, and across its hundred treacherous
miles some dream wilderness, ancient green distances. To stay
would have meant the death by proximities. To have been too
close to her, to the places of us, to an old me. Certain
that going was the only way to leave her, myself, all
that I had to be far from so I could survive even
the obvious threats like winter. After the road
and sea, another road, smaller, a lane perhaps,
up into hills of extinct tribes. Then stone towns
where such innovations as a twentieth century had not
yet been introduced. That was all to the good. In one empty
sandstone house I waited out the smashed foot the foodless days
the loveless months. Borrowed a radio and heard Prokofiev's third
piano concerto. Found another road, lost it again and the hills closed
in. A way of camping in a feedshed, the sleepingbag on high bales
of hay, waking at five to frost, mist, ghostly sheep, and, past
the farm fence, miles from quiet Osterley, an icy baptism in
winter's rivers. Spending a season of this type, meeting
hundreds of strangers, a State, the last land before
the ice age, even her way of smiling through me
or the ache that beach summer cannot quite
dispel faded a little and finally to
return was only a journey, was the
ritual of roads leading to doors
which, though, still remember
not to open to the uncertain
tapping of numb poethands
in the pale season far
from being winter
which I shall
rather term
regret

Before and after

I

we wake with nothing, early, when it is
coldest. the day is a cloud. flick a switch,
fill the room with the fifth brandenburg,
reach for a book. nothing. bees in a belljar
we hum and stir under the immense
weight of romanticism, spring
bursting like ghosts through concrete,
roses, roses. reality would be
bread on a table, and we have no food; illusion
would be drugs, and our supplies
were found by Customs.

to leave or stay, no reason. clouds mass
above us, heavy, the day is sightless
and we sing as the blind sing, so we can
find each other in the dark.

II

this year, for the first time,
the magazines are mirrors, and the bookshop windows
reflect your printed face. timetable:
autograph some copies downtown
address a meeting
go to a stranger's party.
friends drop away, they see the
leeches coming, they leave you to success.

as in the chinese paintings
you go down to the cities
while a few
walk outward separately
pass without recognition

After the party

the evening is gone, and friends. he walks from
room to room, finding
in each relinquished glass
the taste of who has been there. and
and in the final room,
morning and someone sleeping.

Logistics

perhaps they start by instinct;
rising, some to make bread,
some to deliver, all to eat

what they call work
is more habit,
and motive, incentive

there is word for everything
for some things there are several words
and some words
are so perfect .
they require nothing
a habit of characters
existing for itself.

Self-analysis

you tire of it, this
cleverness
there are too many poems
two walls of shelves   a desk
a safe all crammed with poems

your letters turn into poems
your poems into drivel
soon there will be
no-one to write to
then you will claim you are misunderstood

The '69 Coonamble Cup

No rain for months, and then of course
Race Day arrived and down she came:
only ten points, but you can't race on swamp.
They called it off, adjourning to a pub.
Some hours later, arguing the toss:
'We would have won it easy.' 'Break it down!
Transit was home and hosed, no risk.'
So Jack Poletti made a challenge of it—
the Cup for fifty yards down the main street,
with colours up, first past the post the winner.
Took off their shoes and toed the line,
five hundred punters watching from the footpath.
Ted Kennedy stands over six foot high;
Poletti, somewhat shorter, looked a long shot.
The Race Book shows it ... 'John Poletti, footrace,
five two for fifty yards.' And if it rains
he'll crack it, they reckon, for the Melbourne Cup

On hearing the first poet in spring

Mr. Average Poet is in his late
thirties, married, has two and a half
children by one and a half wives,
works as a clerk or schoolteacher,
wishes he had more time to write.
on the train each morning
he takes paper and fountain
pen from his briefcase, glimpses
a river of lilies, a bedroom window,
something of a face, and records
his perceptions of it. he is a good worker
for his employers but sometimes
there is a moment when he stops
working and tries for peace. Has had
one and two thirds volumes published,
gets the occasional invitation, believes
in better critics than he gets. the true
art of our time is something which
desolates.

Suitors

they meet at dawn; stepping from black
carriages in the dim, almost perfect
silence. the woods are empty. even
the birds are silent. the wind
turns over a leaf, there is nothing.
watched by their seconds, they select
weapons; pace the green distance, turn,
shoot at each other. impassive
morning keeps its time. the trees do not
wave their arms about, nor the grass cry.
the coaches drive away.

Chess

for Charles

observations at the end of august, and for a ballet; first,
that the night submerges everything. it begins with a smell of
wine, or that something will happen. blue cruise of police.
the prostitutes move out of sight until the
law is diluted in traffic. tourists mill about.
showcases offer tasseled breasts,
a spotlight of skin, silk, cover charges. violence. drums for her movemen
outside, the wind herds darkness down each lane,
and the clouds push houses over. somehow the moon is lost in a skyful o
lights.

some of the lights stop flashing. the tourists go away, leaving
littered departures. coffeebars catch the homeless in transition.
it seems they have come from nowhere, these men with
nothing to learn. they speak or do not speak.
they drink from the cups before them.

there is an attic room nearby. the poet has brought home a friend, who s
awkwardly in his jeans, unsure of movement.
they touch like rivers. the wind will not disturb them,
or know their loving. like a menial it carries scraps in shadow

distortions. over a skein of alleys the sun is five a.m.
                 it is very precise, it is a flare on a plain of disasters.
                 the cups are empty in the bars &
                      the police run out of victims.
in the attic the walls slope together and meet; in their angle
a thin warm ray funnels toward the sleepers. their heads are close
and bodies tight against cold. if
                              morning is honest

it must be naked like them
in a bare room
where everything is something else
and all the world each other

Living's . . . kind of my hobby (me)

'It is the nature of all mankind to be discontented with prosperity.'
—Aeschylus

its more than we could
change or right
by exchanging reality for symbols
the whole world had been misled.
we cannot help you
our hands are flowers
pity is useless
we will observe
the ways you break
the ways you kill your
children. its sad
but your own work
we'll be the ones who'll
watch the worthless
change hands. By worthless
I mean anything that
requires a sacrifice
we'll watch you
burn each other
steal countries
but don't expect us to
sponsor your
television death

Peter

1

so childhood ends
school's out
the world begins

kensington games
faces
names

amid dull
lectures he
appeared

made some
illicit comment

and afterwards
we met

long hair and beard
old coat
i liked him

hitched to his room
first view of paddington
first smoke   he said
when i was high

i could
do anything with you

i didn't
disagree

2

moved in
first to his room
and then to my own
across the landing

stoned all the time
selling to people
meeting them

listening
to blues
and hum
of the old city

fame from lost
poems scribbled
here and there

3

and he wrote
also

prose

to exercise
the muscles
of his hand

i keep
the best of it

he has forgotten

4

went south
or north
rode into distance

smashed up first week
went off a curve
at 80 miles an hour

to wake in hospital
to pain to morphine

connected
fixed

woke later
in other hospitals

they'd found me
draped in a bathroom

and doors had no keys then

5

there were days
to remember

beds that were full of knees

and night itself
who'd lost her clothes
and did it
for a bet

6

my friends die young
i bring them luck

and none to them
who share my bed

only to grow
or go
or maybe learn

keep endless days
they were too long

only the needle in my arm
or smile
across a pillow

Form

air is replaced by smoke
people become traffic

in the slow
afternoon to evening

evening to night
where falling is invisible

black engines shunt white
or at least pink

in darkness fever grows
like a painful wistaria

the harbour evaporates
we are the yachts

the ferries and sardines
beneath the bridges

the absolute centre of a
civilisation is something which rots

And no bird sings

the music is over
its time now
for silence, for
listening to the wind, the
rain.   say nothing,
that would be wrong, speaking
is words no more, is not poems.
humanity is ghosts and politics,
is hopeless sentiment.

its time now
to say nothing
time for the wind

time for the green pastures
the quiet waters

time for
Cain or a serpent
or a miracle

And no bird sings

autumn breaks on high rocks
fragmentary winter

chimneys, desolation,
brick music towns

footsteps of leaves
& old men's feet
make promises on
midnight roads

the wind's cry
more terrible than silence

I wish the night would speak
or some green fire illumine
the shipwreck of our time

what god will listen to me
sing in the vast
drowning cathedral of a flagon

what cross
bear such guilt
a wasted world

image of a
streetlight in a desert
a tree in a burnt city

going home/the salty taste of
more than sea/the bitter seasons

Sabbath

windy Sunday in Suffolk
Street Hilary and Michael
close like Diogenes lying on pavement

crowds gathered cars took photographs
a cat made its grey
game in our bodies' courtyard

Paddington drowns expensively in white
paint we the loving roll about
dirty ecstatic in a mossy gutter

such an odd word Fornication

as it happened, written

For Hilary, her birthday

rain falls
on itself
each day our room has not changed, not
grown in the night while we slept

a flower grows
in the desert
and our love
surviving in a city

the world is
no more than this

rooms unchanging, cities,
progress to sinister unknowns—
and us, love, a catalyst,
saving the whole

Solitaries

they come here
only
who strain against gravity

they kick away earth, possessions,
wives or husbands, for cool
lovers who are of the wind

drifting
upward together
nothing could slow them

not doubt, not
wishing, nor the thin
skeins of memory

time brings them back
who have passed beyond going—
they fall alone, there being
no-one to wait, to love

and all there was, all
they have learnt
is this sense of flying, the taste
of the high, single winds

blowing for no-one
unaccountably

Rimbaud in Paris

in the still winter he lives
in an overcoat, books in a bag,
his hands in pockets.
freezes. waterpipes ice,

rain drifts to him from windows,
his mouth a diamond of green avenues.
in a rented room, *the poet is the thief
of fire*, writing of wolves and a forest.

pawnshop morning. people, only, are not
secondhand; there is something to learn
from this one's clothes, that's gestures.
the great man of french lit is 17 and has found
that one pair of underpants is not enough.

cafes still tolerate him. in the hague
his contemporary sells prints for a gallery,
scrawls his first charcoal drawings, writes
to his brother. to the poet of new thought

seduction is a secondary pastime; he must convince,
not reassure. the tailor of light, he alters his
pockets to hold a bottle of wine, hands,
a sheaf of colours, fire,
burning a hole in time

Distance

a dry month, a bare month,
a windy month
leaves at my feet
numb hands
and not a song

the sky passes, or the earth;
in the distance
they are burning a forest

and I, a solitary figure,
casting for words to sing with,
day into night, like an
old fisherman, his sign
bones and an empty sail

Today

today is the
childrens regatta

in the street
standing on
forgotten games
they launch their
white yachts
into a rainstream

hours later
when they are called home
only their bodies go

their spirit far away
trembling on the current
in boats of paper, poems

Trees
for Hilary

felt good
that night
made it
later
she saw
my astral body
leaning above her
in the still dark

two of us woke
next day
oatmeal walls white sun

goodtimes
walking through countries
eating toward each other
through an apple

fasting on hilltop
wearing what i see

writing what i know
        that the wind has said it
        that the sky reflects the mind

inventing little
& only to patch
memory's empty spaces

Cicuta Maculata

they lie between white sheets
touching each other's
pale as winter skin

some words are said
whose syllables congeal
the ears drift up with sleep

the civic orchestra floats by
clinging to drums and 'cellos
the conductor is learning to swim

in a cathedral
the stale flesh of last sunday's lord
bobs on the nun-dark water

how well the flowers will grow
next year
between the cobbles

it rains
all over town
in the dim evening

through flooded streets
a noah's ark assortment
of the dead

hard to tell
enemy from friend
in so much night

the faces of the drowning
swell like bosch faces
synthesis of blue and red

the lovers drift on
separate currents now
fucked like leander

dress quickly by the fire for soon
its light will show us what we are
—not dancers in corroborees
we had imagined in the incense sky
and not the wakers on a chaste
high balcony above Verona

seagods who drown in seeking out
the nature of their medium
their arms drilled through with misled pilgrimmage
their eyes a pageant of defeat's emotions
their faces sallow tender and betrayed
—captives of a no longer magic kingdom

two in a cold and silenced and
embittered morning carpeted with fragments
of last night's savage paradise
—addiction leaves its haunted wrack
below the tideline of ideals
like prayers that fall on stony ground

The poets dream of making films

if moments had the weight of gulls
singing would deafen us   your hands
making crab tracks across me without
even a beach to justify their trip

for us time is immense we are characters
already taking our places in a frieze of time
and history   we touch again lying together
we fit together well   your voice falters
as though the pages were uncut

we have read many books about the navigations
it spoils us for the sea   only
brilliant coy images of waves and shore escape

everything i have ever seen burns in the retina
across distance through bedroom skies and gullcries

i lie on my back now finished watching for
stars which fall without motive and to aid no
charities

Free horror

disappointed in love
he turns to his winter
circus of gay woebegone
clowns and his animals trained
also to walk gravely
upright   their front legs held
out in a sort of greeting   dismembers
a jew or two   feeds them to the geeks
an elephant stands about   has forgotten
something   lions pad among children
lord god who runs his circus well
owns two top hats and a skin
for ceremonies   his cripples
advertise the show   he has thought of everything
each night he has a different jester   those
who displease are eaten by their friends

Fleshback

    direct light
warps it   keep in a cool
place   this side up   avoid
shaking   her hand is a starfish
or   how green the los angeles
sun   two thirds of the city
already   with a leaf
a flake of stone
unaspiring   came back to grain
of wood 'honest surfaces' or
how each is a leaf or three
unidentical characters

the action of a particular
starfish is multiplied by its
tribes which assemble at one end
of a reef of coral maybe
a mile deep and fix on it
leaving pale bones as of
eaten mermaids & eat
their way to the end

each item now lucent under
soft light watch fingers move
they are really quite
intricate
and see how in the centre
soft ridges quiver try to form
sentences

definite movement   call it
baroque   three characters

cut deep perhaps a mile such
cute calligraphy & wants to be
in the movies but is starting
its career with a little
modelling
under a microscope

For Anne so still and dreamy

taking it in turns to connect
I'd hit the street one day
or she'd drive up on doctors
get a 'script burn down a chemist

for a few months we lived
a flower at a time

time was
outside our circle

fixing fixing
arms eaten with punctures
the room a Chaos a subjective
junkyard

last week, I think on Tuesday,
she died
just gave up breathing
toppled over
a big smashed doll
with the needle still in her arm

I made a funeral of leaves
and sang the Book of Questions
to her face as white as hailstones
to her eyes as closed as heaven

stone breasts and decomposing smile
she died first
it was her turn

119

Revision

Time has bound me
by so many threads and veins
to what must pass for death.
Fills my songs with desolate
images, ghosts and ruins, cold,
cold, the features of a skeleton,
the logic of a nightmare.
What shall they deduce from it?
Lost in himself, his dreams, they'll say,
drank too much wine, and had a country house.

Cassandra too

funeral music / nothing is true /
and so much left undone
the room a block of ice with shapes
which seem to move   which seem to be
nothing matters / yes / more drugs
we are in our own camp
the air is frozen but the house is mine.

O all these books   all these musics
all they say and do not say
I'd swap the lot for darkness, for oblivion
Overdose is a congenial exit
no effort is required
rain in our hair dries salty damp
no food no warmth no future

lets go like this, with friends too far away
and never care how different could be
the weeping garden where the stone flowers hide.

Psalm

Night besieges me.
The blackout curtains and barricades
are in position, no-one will disturb me
in this bomb-shelter.

I have sent them away,
bored with their deceit;
if they come they will find
nothing but a haunter,

nametags left in a cloakroom
ten unpublished books some letters
the possessions one acquires
on a visit to this planet.

Vicissitude keeps sharp
the adze I think with;
memory amuses me a little,
like a gas-chamber filled with errors.

No forwarding address

Weary and alone, beaten by the bitter
ease of it all,
falling faster than a falling
star
for
stars burn, they can be seen,
some have occupied
celestial satrapies.
It is dark, I am desolate, the
memories hurtle past and I do not
reach for them, they would
break my hand and already
too much has broken in my hand;
so many things, dead because I
disclosed them to the shadows.
I never made a song of the silence
but it doesn't matter.
Most of my
friends
have vanished, I searched everywhere—
but they were gone, leaving no word.
Those who did not vanish
do not know me
I am a stranger
thin and devil-haunted. Songs I knew
have not been sung since it began,
when once needing you
I called and you heard and did not come
but falsely left me to the unkind wind
and the paid assassins of winter; later
upon the bleak impassable
escarpment of withdrawal

as I clung to stay sane while my
world was ablaze and crucificial
there was no sign that you
even remembered me.

I wasted, pacing out the ramshackle
captivity of a
camp for displaced Romantics.
Now its almost winter again
this may be my last chance to
talk to you ...
you do not listen.

The war is over
some of the soldiers
will not be coming home.

Poem about the sun   & new
poems   Yesterday   i begin
the sun most often
a flare in a grey parachute   Today
the same   but just now has broken through
Warms me   typing by a window   institutional
food   We could laugh all day and get nothing
done   Wouldn't be the first time
When the cat comes sit on you
work stops   But here in the open landscape
there's no commitments   Nothing to be done
Here in the grey country   green
last week   Chameleon country   could be
keats   The sun is allotted to everyone   even
poor people   or especially, have no roof
to keep the flies off   Dreams
has lunched   sleeps
with the sporting pages over his face
to keep the flies off   Dreams
sometimes   illogically   With new clothes
going baggy   With money in the pocket
incipient cancer

In the studio milk stands about
on the table   We are designing
yellow helmets   Tags to be worn
at functions   Designing the great office party
Rubber steaks made from cartyres   floormats
exoil cocktails   Scrip napkins   The present
lasts a decade   it was grey
before that   dimly remembered
in old cars   The future is how much
we don't fuck up   Now it seems

minimal   I could live on cakes
when the bread runs out   thats possible

II

Programmatic   Problems of measurement   Computes
new style fifth year doomed plans surprises
Remarkable   If it were fibergrass
it would be no surer   Comes   Goes   Intricacies
of the domestic view/ & philosophers   Last chance
for the perplexed & viewless   Soon
the next phase   Robot riser   each day the same
More open space   Recreational taut areas   As
branches play in a given arc from their stem
at play in its arc   Stem climbing to a given
height from preset earth   The tree squad   Birdlike
throwaway lines of country closed to deer & wildfowl
Cityplaces   And how
arcs of cyberstructure close out   form strange
refute weather   Refute
ultimately   their own small warp and strike

III

if he spoke at all he would use short words. cut
back to senses. says nothing. shows lightly.

parallels.
dependant

only on grace. moves,
also, lightly, as

a gull carries herself, or a moth. the real
centre of what moves is still. the true

centre of art is yellow. or blue. or glows
redly, embers. or is cold. thinks

or is orange, like the blood of a maple, and
feels.

The image school, or, weather report from veriest parnassus

stars shatter the window/their ancient
    wisdom/the mysteries/horology of
brown leaves dead when the rain sets in

wind catching at lutestring reeds, old
    minstrel

my brown house a city of white insects

symmetry of waves? metric of tides? rather
    that things invisible have set the shore in patterns

lastly, i suppose, make message of birds singing, or
    say the bread-van's creaking wheels sound
like the lost plays of dante

Death of a blowfly

beat yourself to death
on this invisible

christ it is
'shot while trying...'

you are etched on this
lacemaker's landscape
on the detectives' boots
stitched by informers
whisperers

they grow rich on innocence
they didn't do it
not them

your eyes sewn closed
by a coroner
a sailmaker

they smile
look the other way

small men with knives

Outing

   national waters   & for the beaches
shabby waves collapse   conjunctions
of ocean   grey pier   disinterest
is centred on the groups standing
about   from nowhere to this   from this
to subside on coal sand   national coast
of skint scrape clothes   jaunty the way
the wind takes cliffs in one easy
curve   blows the boats over   the kids
piss in their sea clothes & the shore
grows older under ice cream papers too
grey to look like snow   the true
centre of time is something
which rots

Assignation

we will meet
where we always do
go where we go
we will talk and he will
undress me then himself
he will touch me everywhere
with his sea hands
our two mouths wed
burst inside each other
lie late together
we will part
where we always do

The rodeurs

they are glum
its certain

have stared
through a thousand
sea storms

lies on her side   they
watch her

skulls on pillars

keats
their sad sage
yellows

have stared
too long

   they would sing
if they had no wings

But reach instead
for that soft river
under her gown

SOUNDGRaphs—for
TIM JOHNSON

while your hand that
i used to know glides

meaningfully over
paper a truck

struggles up the hill
a door bangs

a bird sings

and you graph
activities   grasp

antiquities

V.R.

they're dying now
not that they ever lived

childhoods weeping in ghostly
victorian lavatories

all they made well
survives them

their wars have been cleaned up
mud's dried to history

black words
yellowed pages

their children age
talk wisely

or find them
under a stone in the country

Exhumations

1

the house stood
under pine
above a river
birds dived

watch them fall
rise with a fish

fires were
peopled

to the north
we were

fumbling
a war

2

or see them hang
(clouds? eagles?

heroes? a road train
haltingly trailing   stop

while the man
descends

and goes about
prodding his cattle

to their feet as one should
stand before execution

3

five hundred
miles was

not enough
from campbell st

and squads
would come

driving that way
through drought or rain

to visit me
break in its a

bust

4

trees watched
them   fires

breaking the fine
line of a windbreak

wheatfields burning
red as vincent

birds swung away
rabbits   these stood

perhaps to green
again or be gaunt

for the photographers

their nature is to stand
defenceless you will not hear them

cry

5

once a black
lady came

to read
her verses

she had set her people
down in a pamphlet

the words were black or course
in creamy reams

cawed for them
through a giggle of pentameter

through a blush of rhyme
through sales and royalties

better to give them land
than sherries with the cwa

and autographs in
book week

the dances

sections of the music to be displayed to the audience

a bent clarinet   tangle of piano   trodden lute

a short-order band plays with instruments of hair bone & gut

the dancers appear   they would be naked but the day is cold & wear
cobwebs & harlequin   they would be dancing but have forgotten how t
move

stunned film   clubbed seals on white icecap   baby harvest   golgotha
village in asia   heaps of bodies   predominant colours are bloodred
smokeblack   uniformed liberators free the villagers from living

someone has painted a nipple on the dome of the white house
and round the door   two buttocks

the dancers leave   somewhere they
find a wood   it comes to life as the tribe carves flutes from bamboo &
the dance begins   loss of memory   sections of the music   sun on
clearwater   paths drowned in leaves   skinpoems

John Francis Dransfield

life
refined by suffering
is art

there are no artists

only
who love
who suffer

around them
light

for my father
died this night
26. XI. 1971

Notes

p. 26 This poem, posthumously published in *Meanjin* as "the piano like Monk or Bogart" was originally called "First Casino poem" as it appears here—and was written when the poet worked in Casino, NSW, on the local newspaper.

p. 31 In explanation of the word 'saturated' (stanza 7, line 2), the original sketch for this poem had the line 'Vodka a saturated puppet'.

p. 39 In manuscript this poem, 'Desert fragment' was coupled with 'Paragraph in the style of Stephane Mallarme' published in *Streets of the Long Voyage*.

p. 67 Line 7 in the typescript has 'hugh', I have read this as 'high' rather than 'huge'.

p. 70 Cocklebiddy. Perhaps from 'cockabondy', in turn from the Welsh *Coch a bon ddu,* an angling term for an artificial fly of a fancy kind. The Welsh means 'red with black trunk'. Cocklebiddy is a small stopping place on the Nullarbor Plain.

p. 77 The manuscript carries the comment, 'c.f. the legend of the Flying Dutchman'.

p. 123 Line 8 in the typescript has 'strapies', which I have read as 'satrapies', and line 32 has 'escapment' which I have read as 'escarpment'.

p. 140 The context of the poem would suggest the title should read "the dancers", but the only copy I have to hand reads "the dances".

Appendix A

Disgorging all this as three drafts of one poem; the first, stimulated by first-hearing much of Satie's piano music. Considering the times, Paris, its poets. Re-typing it, changed much, retained both drafts; retyping second, improvised, imagining in the portrait a mirror, and its differing reflections of sixty years ago. Moralising, reacting, telling, asking. Camus wrote:' By the treatment the artist imposes upon reality, he declares the intensity of his rejection of it.' I am learning what that means. These three drafts indicate my selection and rejection of material, thought-sequences, assimilations, all written in a period of some hours, although the total writing time would be no more than fifteen minutes.

Michael Dransfield, 21.III.1969

One cannot photograph a fantasy
unless someone will act it out.
Heap of pianos, the rubble of creative solitude,
two hundred umbrellas opening like nightward flowers
colourful in lonely hallucinations,
what a richness of bluntly mystic
austerity he endured, dissembling
fierce suicides in utter otherness.
Did he find that discerningly
being Satie meant quite involving
years in compassionless alleys of harmonic
freakout* ? And, endful as Murger or the street-painter**,
what autobiographies did he not diffuse
through the white-keys garret of kaleidoscope soul?
Fools stop smiling this is no Calvary to laugh at !!
(*freakout = ingenuity. **Maurice Utrillo)

II

One cannot photograph a fantasy
unless someone will act it out;
 and was it only that, or a cave painting in a room above the city,
 a man and his ideals; for him writing was
 bringing up a lost child into ideals and above all these new-seeing
 eyes, as one would wander openeyed in a temple to Beauty at Sparta
 if there were one; surprised to find him at work creative in a country at wa
 always; huns on the borders, or the sea, or commerce, or distractions;
 he and Gaudier Brzeska; others ? perhaps Debussy, or the unknown poet.
 But from the other side of atomic warfare, how are we to see it but as fant
 as 'venturing earliest music*' rediscovered. Unreal as Rossetti, seemingly.
 Satie, his heap of pianos, the rubble of constructive solitude,
 two hundred umbrellas opening like flowers
 colourful for lonely hallucination transcripted faithfully,
 what a richness of bluntly mystic
 austerity he endured, atoning christlike for true vision,
 dissembling fierce suicides in utter otherness.
 Did he find that living his karma
 meant quite involving years
 in compassionless alleys of harmonic
 freakout ? And, endful as Murger or the street painter,
 what autobiographies did he not diffuse
 through the white-keys garret of kaleidoscope soul, a map for future yoyage

(*Rilke, from first Duino elegy)

III

One cannot understand another's fantasy
until it has been acted out.
And was it only that, or a cave painting in a room above a city,
a man and his ideas; for him writing music was

ging up a child into ideals and above all those new-seeing
, eyes that might wander open-eyed as in the Louve, comprehending;
nishing to find him at work creative in a country at war
ys; huns at the borders, and the sea, and prosperities, and distractions;
nd Gaudier-Brzeska: others ? Debussy perhaps, or the unknown soldier.
from the dark age of Hiroshima, how are we to see it but as fantasy,
enturing earliest music', unreal like Rossetti, seemingly, a fable
by captor Muses to perplex us. For what reason ? Doubt takes us nowhere.
etain a legend. The scene is a garret, a pile of pianos, a cafe, a weird
                                                  collection.
as a child, but who has put away childish things
handful of maps of some Richard Jefferies place
dremt of, escaped to, longed for, until utopia poisons the system
the brutal fact of impossibility. Tantalus. Improvisations carefully
ing us by the hand into the great forest, goliards, pilgrims, fools, who is to
e us, we who listen, attend these teachings ?
portrait becomes a mirror I disappear into its sequences the day a cadenza
curiosity an eye on a stalk, a sessile eye, believing.
g him would have meant changing all he saw unconsciously, replacing
                                        picturesque
ls with fantastic imagery. All real enough. But one shellburst has landed
close, it is all breaking, nothing will last, all we celebrate is that
ved, this was he, what he did, APPARENTLY.

Appendix B

Key to year of composition. An asterisk indicates that the date has been surmised on the basis of text, context or style.

1967

No forwarding address
The card game

1968

Desert fragment
First Casino poem
Richmond River

1969

*Afternoon
And all the world
Arcangelo (more and more of late)
Astatlot
Cafe society
Camelot lane
Cassandra too
Chaconne for a solipsist
Differencias
Dress quickly by the fire
*Duet
For Ann so still and dreamy
Going away
Hangover
July the nineteenth, 1969
Lonely as a cloud
*Memoirs

And no bird sings (autumn breaks on high rocks)
And no bird sings (the music is over)
Arcangelo (where the hill falls tidal)
Becoming *sky*
Before the hour of streetlights
Birch trees, Courland Penders
Chess
Cicuta Maculata
'dear Charles'
Death as triumph
Distance
Falling asleep in snow
For Charles Blackman
Form
Grandfather
Hands
'if life were love'
Illness
Imaginary wife and lover
In the high country
In the park
Island farm
*Living's...kind of my hobby (me)
On hearing the first poet in spring
Philosophy of movement
Potato-land
Presences
Small
Stalin-style
*Suitors
Surrexit Dominus
The dances
The dinner hour
The face in the mirror
The sun but not our children

To the colour red
Trees

1971

Assignation
Before and after
*Death of a blowfly
*Exhumations
Fleshback
For Hilary, her birthday
Free horror
'I want my paintings to be comfortable armchairs'
John Francis Dransfield
Logistics
Outing
Peter
Poem about the sun
Rimbaud in Paris
Solitaries
Soundgraphs
The image school, or, weather report from veriest parnassus
The poets dream of making films
The rodeurs
Third seer's tale
Today
V.R.

Poems for which no date of composition is yet known

Bum's Rush II. Through the ice
Chopin: the winter wind
'Height above height it rises'
Journal d'un homme vide (my watch is slowing now)
Journal d'un homme vide (Three Aprils ago)
When her last poems